Light to live by

Right to live by

Light to live by

Readings in John's Gospel

Alistair Hornal
Susan Penfold
Claire Powell
Ro Willoughby

Editor: Ro Willoughby

Inter-Varsity Press

INTER-VARSITY PRESS
38 De Montfort Street, Leicester LE1 7GP, England

First published under the title Start here *in 1988*
This revised edition 1997

British Library Cataloguing in Publication Data
A catalogue record for this book is available from the British
Library.

ISBN 0-85111-197-1

Set in Cheltenham and Franklin Gothic

Typeset in Great Britain by Textype Typesetters, Cambridge

Printed in Great Britain by The Guernsey Press Co. Ltd,
Guernsey, Channel Islands

Inter-Varsity Press is the book-publishing division of the
Universities and Colleges Christian Fellowship (formerly the
Inter-Varsity Fellowship), a student movement linking Christian
Unions in universities and colleges throughout the United
Kingdom and the Republic of Ireland, and a member movement
of the International Fellowship of Evangelical Students. For
information about local and national activities write to UCCF,
38 De Montfort Street, Leicester LE1 7GP.

Contents

Foreword

Deciding to be a follower of the Lord Jesus Christ is the most important choice you could ever make. It is a decision that needs to be followed through in the ups and downs of everyday living. The New Testament has a word that sums up this process – *discipleship*. A disciple is someone who is a devoted learner, and that involves commitment of our minds, our emotions and our wills.

Followers of Jesus in every generation have found that dedicated study of the Bible is one of the ways to grow as a disciple. The Bible, which is often referred to as 'the Word of God', helps to shape our lives according to God's pattern. That is why, as a Christian determined to follow Jesus, you need to seize every opportunity to hear the Bible clearly taught and explained.

But simply hearing more experienced Christians teaching the Bible message is not enough. God wants us to learn to read his Word for ourselves, and to develop the skill of allowing the Holy Spirit to speak into our own lives on a daily basis.

Light to live by has been produced to help you to do just that in a personal way. This book comprises six weeks of representative studies on the message of John's Gospel, as a gateway to the New Testament and the whole Bible. Through these devotional studies you will begin to get to grips with some important truths:

- Who is Jesus?
- What is the significance of his death on the cross?
- What does it mean to have the Holy Spirit living in my life?
- How can I learn to pray?
- How can I grow as a follower of Christ?

As you follow the studies through day by day, not only will you begin to gain a clearer understanding of the Christian faith but also the questions and comments will help you to apply these truths to different areas of your life.

Human beings are creatures of habit. Making up your mind to be a disciple of Jesus means dropping old habits that do us no good and learning new ones that will help us to grow in our faith. *Light to live by* is designed to get you established in the habit of spending time each day learning from God as you study the Bible.

Francis Bacon wrote, 'Some books are to be tasted, others to be swallowed, and some few to be chewed and digested.' As you set out on these studies, the aim is to help you to chew and digest the Word of God, to make it part of your life, to renew your mind and bring you an understanding of God's heart for the world.

I hope you enjoy reading *Light to live by* and using it to take you into the book that is above all books ... the book which will change your life.

July 1997

Ian Coffey
Plymouth

Introduction

So you have decided to live your life as a Christian. Have you had so many new experiences and ideas that sometimes you feel a juggler – keeping all the balls in the air with a sneaking fear that you could drop the lot? You certainly don't want to do that. And what about all this talk of reading the Bible and letting God speak directly to you through it?

If you have heard it said that the Bible is God's word to us today, as true now as it was centuries ago, then you have heard correctly. But you can discover that this is true for you too. As you explore the Bible for yourself you will come to know God in a very personal way. Many of your cherished ideas could be questioned, and the new ideas you are encountering will come into clearer focus. But God wants you to understand, and His Spirit will help you at all times. So don't fret about potentially being labelled a 'juggler in disgrace'!

Rather, you may soon come to share these sentiments of the author John White, in his book *The Fight*:

Bible study has torn apart my life and remade it. That is to say that God, through his Word, has done so. In the darkest periods of my life when everything seemed hopeless, I would struggle in the grey dawns of many faraway countries to grasp the basic truths of Scripture passages. I looked for no immediate answers to my problems. Only did I sense intuitively that I was drinking drafts from a fountain that gave life to my soul.

Ro Willoughby

About this book

Light to live by is designed to help you to explore the Bible through John's Gospel – a book uniquely suited to beginners and more weathered Christians alike. It is written specially for those who are determined to follow in Jesus' footsteps. The book is split up into six sections or weeks, each containing five studies. Each section should take five days to complete and is followed by a suggested Bible reading for the weekend. At the end of each week you will find short and helpful explanations of some of the key points of the Christian faith and how they affect the way we live.

Each study should take up to half-an-hour to complete, although you can take as long as you have available. You might even like to go through them with someone who has been a Christian for a longer time than yourself, someone who could help explain things.

You will find that various approaches to Bible reading have been adopted. One week, for example, we are looking at people whom Jesus met; in another week we are reading longer sections of John's Gospel to get a bird's-eye view of the last days of Jesus' life; another week is spent entirely in meditating on just one chapter. We are concentrating on John's Gospel but not exclusively. So there is plenty of variety. But the basic approach is the same – to find out what a portion of the Bible is saying, and then to apply its meaning to us as followers of Jesus, living on the verge of a new millennium.

You are encouraged to do a bit of thinking and writing for yourself. You might like to use a notebook

11

of your own or use the spaces left in each study and make your notes there. Writing down your thoughts helps to clarify your thinking.

These studies will also lead you to prayer – either thanking God for who he is and what he has done, or asking him to act in situations where you or others need his help. There may be times when you want to ask for forgiveness too. So try to make time for prayer before, after and during each study.

The hope and prayer of the writers of this book is that by using this material you will be helped to lay enduring foundations for your life as a follower of Jesus. We hope that this will be the gateway to a lifetime of discovery, finding that God does actually speak to you through the Bible. He speaks in such a way that, if you obey him, your own life will become more and more in line with Jesus' life. What greater goal in life could anyone have than to become like the greatest person who has ever walked on this earth – Jesus Christ – God become a human being?

WHO IS JESUS?

A detailed study

A t the centre of the Christian faith is a man who is also God: the Lord Jesus Christ. He alone can forgive sin. He alone can give people the right to become children of God. And there is so much more that he alone can do.

John's Gospel goes right to the heart of this remarkable mystery: that in Jesus God has become a human person. Without any preamble, he 'plunges you in at the deep end' with some of the greatest things written about anyone: truths that could either blow your mind or cause you to bow before this unique Person in wonder and worship. Let the full significance of these truths dawn on you as John unfolds the answer to the key question: WHO IS JESUS?

This week we shall be looking at the first two chapters of John's Gospel in detail. As you read the few verses for each day's study, ask yourself what the most important things are that John is saying. Then let God help you to relate them to your own life and circumstances.

1. Jesus in relationship to God

John 1: 1-18

What a build-up! John's Gospel opens with a glowing description of someone whose identity is only made completely clear in verse 17.

1. *What word pictures and descriptive phrases does John use to tell us about Jesus Christ? Read through John 1: 1-18 and list them. Alongside each write down what ideas these words conjure up in your mind.*

_____

_____

_____

_____

_____

2. *Jesus is described as 'the Word'. What does that suggest about him? How does this help you to understand who he is (a) in relation to God, and (b) in relation to you? (See verses 1-3 and 14 especially, and write down what you find.)*

_____

_____

_____

_____ _____

_____ _____

3. *Without words we would often be in the dark about what people were thinking and would find it difficult to get to know other people. How does God let us know himself? What does 'the Word' tell us about God that we would not otherwise know? (Begin by looking at verses 16-18, then go back over the whole passage.)*

_____

_____

_____

_____

_____

God knows all that we say and do. He even knows what we are thinking! But it is often helpful to put our thoughts into words. As you have thought about who the Lord Jesus Christ is during your study today, turn your thoughts into words in a prayer of thanks and worship in appreciation of Jesus.

There are some obvious similarities between the opening words of John's Gospel and the opening words of the Bible. If you have time, read Genesis 1 and then think again about what you have learned about Jesus and God from John chapter 1.

2. Jesus in relationship to John the Baptist

John 1: 19-34

John the Baptist (a different person from the John who wrote the Gospel) clearly made a great impact – people naturally wanted to know who he was. Lest there be any possible doubt, he makes it quite clear who he was *not* (verses 19-23). In contrast to himself, he points out who Jesus is.

1. *A witness is someone who tells the truth about someone else. (It carries the idea of giving evidence in a law court.) Go over John 1:1-36 and write down what John the Baptist, as a witness, tells us about Jesus.*

The 'I am' sayings in John's Gospel

An interesting study in John's Gospel would be to go through the many occasions where Jesus uses the phrase 'I am' with a particular concept following. So in 6:35 he says, 'I am the bread of life …'; in 8:12, 'I am the light of the world'. The other main places to find these are:

10:7, 11	the door; the good shepherd
11:25	the resurrection and the life
14:6	the way, the truth and the life
15:1	the true vine

As you look these up ask yourself *why* Jesus used these names of himself and what significance they have.

'I am' would have rung bells in the minds of Jewish listeners, since it is very close to the special name they used for God, of LORD or Yahweh. Each time Jesus said this it was as if he was equating himself with God (that is probably why they tried to stone him in 8:58).

_____

_____

_____

2. *John clearly views Jesus as more important than himself (see verses 15 and 25-30). What does this show you about Jesus?*

_____

_____

_____

_____

3. *John the Baptist is not the only witness to Jesus in this section of the Bible. How was John himself left in no doubt that Jesus is the Son of God? (See verses 32-34.)*

_____

_____

_____

_____

One of the most difficult facts to grasp about God is that there is only one true God – and yet he is at the same time three distinct personalities. Here we see the *Holy Spirit of God* bearing witness to *Jesus, the Son of God* – who in turn makes *God the Father* known to us. Don't expect to be able to understand this – as Christians, we worship a God who is far greater than our very limited minds! But we need to accept the Bible's evidence that Father, Son and Holy Spirit are indeed one God.

Note: The studies about the Holy Spirit later in this book will help you towards a better understanding of God.

When you realize just how great God is, the only possible response is to acknowledge your own weakness and bow before him, however high or low an opinion you may have of yourself. Take some time to get your life into a new perspective as you acknowledge that God is far more important than you. As you pray, tell God that Jesus is Lord – and that you want to serve him.

3. Jesus in relationship to the disciples

John 1:35-51

The Baptist's great role was to prepare the way for Jesus (see verse 23) and he had the privilege of introducing Jesus to others, including those who had been his own followers.

1. *How does John introduce Jesus in verse 36? Write down what you think this means in the light of verse 29.*

Note: The Lamb of God: You can find some of the background to this idea in Exodus 12: 3-13 and Isaiah 53 in the Old Testament.

_____

_____

_____

_____

2. *Read through verses 35-51 and write down the different titles given to Jesus or ways in which he is described. What do these words mean? (If you are not sure, look them up in a Bible Dictionary – or ask a more experienced Christian to help you find out.)*

_____

_____

_____

_____

_____

_____

3. *How did the following people find out who Jesus was:*

■ *Andrew?*
■ *Simon?*
■ *Philip?*
■ *Nathanael?*

Make a note of what you discover about each.

_____

_____

_____

_____

_____

_____

_____

Different people come to know Jesus in various ways. How did you encounter Jesus? (It is worth writing down your own story and highlighting the most significant events. Perhaps you will be able to introduce another person to Jesus soon – and your own story may well be of help.)

Take time to thank the Lord Jesus for his invitation to 'follow me' – and to say thanks for any who pointed out to you that Jesus was the Lamb of God (like John) or who brought you to Jesus (like Andrew did for Peter or Philip for Nathanael). Then start to think about whom *you* could introduce to Jesus, and ask God for his help in this.

4. Jesus in relationship to his mother and disciples

John 2: 1-12

Read through these verses.

1. *How does Jesus' response to his mother in verse 4 strike you? Is it what you would expect from him? Why do you think Jesus speaks to her in this way?*

_____

_____

_____

_____

The words 'my hour has not yet come' run like a refrain through John's Gospel – until 12: 23 when Jesus says, '*The hour has come* for the Son of Man to

20

be glorified'. He is referring to the cross. The ultimate demonstration of Jesus' glory lay ahead; even Mary had to realize more fully why Jesus had come into the world.

2. *When problems cropped up, Mary knew that Jesus was able to do something about them. She also knew that whatever he said would work! What can you learn from this incident about the relationship between faith, prayer and obedience?*

_____

_____

_____

_____

_____

3. *Verse 11 describes this miraculous event as a 'sign'. This is John's distinctive word to refer to Jesus' supernatural acts. A sign points to a reality beyond itself; it is full of significance. What does this sign point out about Jesus? What effect did it have on his disciples?*

_____

_____

_____

_____

_____

As you read about Jesus in John's Gospel – all he said and did – let the full impact strike you. It is only as you get to know Jesus (as Mary had over many years and as his disciples were beginning to) that you will really be able to trust him about everything.

The Lord Jesus cares about everything that concerns or worries you. In one sense, running out of wine at a wedding was a major social disaster – although, compared to other problems you may have to face, it could seem small. But however big or apparently trivial your problems are, God invites you to:

Cast all your anxiety on him because he cares for you.

1 Peter 5:7

Signs and miracles in John

John relates seven miracles of Jesus, representative of his ministry, which he calls 'signs':

2:1-11	Water becomes wine
4:46-54	The nobleman's son is healed
5:1-9	The lame man is healed
6:1-14	Feeding of the five thousand
6:16-21	Walking on the water
9:1-12	The blind man is healed
11:1-46	Lazarus is raised

The resurrection is seen as the greatest sign. John relates these miracles at length and with each one there is teaching to explain it. So, as Jesus miraculously feeds the five thousand, he speaks afterwards of himself as 'the bread of life'. The sign and the word of explanation go together. When you have time, study these carefully. These 'signs' are not merely evidence of Jesus' divine power, but they show that he is sent by God and authenticate him as the Son of God and Messiah.

Do that just now. Bring any problems you have to Jesus in prayer. Make up your mind to trust him to take care of them – and to do what he says.

5. Jesus in relationship to the religious establishment

John 2: 13-25

Reading through verses 13-17, it is hardly what you would expect from a 'gentle Jesus, meek and mild'! But then, perhaps that description of Jesus is inadequate. Nor do you see in Jesus that prototype of the 'TV vicar': he is not a model of religious orthodoxy. He comes across rather as someone fired with enthusiasm for everything to do with God.

What was going on in the temple was hardly what you would expect either. The religious people had turned a place which was devoted to the service of God into a supermarket! As you will see, Jesus was quite prepared to 'rock the boat' a bit. With the Son of God on the scene, established religion was in for a shock.

1. *Why do you think Jesus took such forceful action in the temple? Can you imagine the impact it would have on those who were themselves supposed to set an example by their life and worship? What does it show you about Jesus' character and values? Make a note of what you find.*

_____

_____

_____

What is a 'Gospel'?

At first sight, it would be easy to take the four Gospels (the books written by Matthew, Mark, Luke and John which are found at the beginning of the New Testament) as biographies of Jesus. While there is some truth in that, they are different from most biographies and rather more than biographies!

For a start, the Gospels are very selective in what they record. You can see why they have to be selective when you read the last verse of John's Gospel:

> *Jesus did many other things as well. If every one of them were written down, I suppose that even the whole world would not have room for the books that would be written.*

And yet, the Gospel writers (or 'evangelists' as they are often called) were not random in their choice of what to include and what to leave out. Each of the four accounts of Jesus' life brings out distinctive emphases. John, in particular, brings out the significance of what Jesus said and did. His story is certainly not an unbiased factual record, although his facts are accurate, but then he doesn't claim that it is such a record!

> *Jesus did many other miraculous signs in the presence of his disciples, which are not*

recorded in this book. But these are written that you may believe that Jesus is the Christ, the Son of God, and that by believing you may have life in his name.

John 20: 30-31

John's Gospel is a book written from a position of committed faith in Jesus – with the clear intention of inspiring faith in him. What John (as one of the Lord Jesus' best friends) has seen and heard in Jesus has convinced him that Jesus is no ordinary person, but the Son of God and the Saviour of all who believe in him. He wants to pass on the benefit of what he has discovered to everyone who reads his Gospel.

As you read through John's Gospel, try to pay special attention to what Jesus says and does. Look out for times when Jesus himself says, 'I am …'. (You may like to note these sayings down or underline them in your Bible – see page 16.) Notice the meaning John gives to Jesus' miracles (or 'signs' as John calls them – see page 22) and the teaching that goes with them. Above all, read the Gospel prayerfully, asking God every time you pick it up to help you to get to know Jesus better and to grow in your trust in him.

The Greek word which we translate as 'gospel' could be quite literally translated as 'good news'. Our word 'gospel' is an Old English word, *godspel*, literally meaning 'glad tidings'. That's what the Gospels are: Good News Books.

Enjoy reading John's Good News.

_____

_____

2. *Read verses 18-25. Clearly verse 18 is a demand by the Jewish leaders for some authentication of Jesus' authority to do what he had done. What 'sign' did he offer them? What did he mean by this?*

_____

_____

_____

_____

The resurrection is one of the clearest signs of who Jesus is. The apostle Paul writes that he was 'declared *with power* to be the Son of God by his resurrection from the dead' (Romans 1: 4, my italics).

By raising Jesus from death, God vindicated his Son – in the face of the religious establishment. The resurrection was also to continue as one of the central planks in the preaching of the early Christians – a constant source of irritation for the religious authorities. Read Acts 3: 1-4, 22 to discover one such incident.

3. *How important was the fact of the resurrection in Peter's preaching?*

_____

_____

_____

_____

26

4. *What was the reaction of these religious leaders to (a) Peter and John's conviction that Jesus had been raised to life? and (b) their subsequent confident behaviour?*

_____

_____

_____

_____

_____

5. *How does the fact of the resurrection affect your faith in Jesus and your behaviour?*

_____

_____

_____

_____

Sadly, it is possible to have an initial attraction to Jesus and belief in him without having known a life-changing experience of being 'born again'. (Jesus talks about this in John 3, as we shall see in the first day's study next week.) Jesus looks for genuine conversation: a real change in us. He knows us inside out: there is no way that we can deceive him.

Weekend

It is good to read large sections of the Bible in one sitting. To be serious about following him, it is important that you begin to get a grasp of the life and activity of Jesus. So we suggest that, over the next five weeks, you read several chapters of a gospel at one time. If you want to read more than the suggested amount, then go ahead!

This weekend find time to read John, chapters 1-5.

Memory verse: 'Yet to all who received him, to those who believed in his name, he gave the right to become children of God' (John 1:12).

A new start!

So you are a Christian! Perhaps this has happened very recently. Everything is different; it's a whole new world to enter and understand ...

For some, becoming a Christian happens gradually over a period of time; others can point to a very specific date. For some it is a quiet dawning of truth and change of mind and life, while others go through a dazzling experience that is the spiritual equivalent of Blackpool illuminations! Some come from religious backgrounds and others know nothing beforehand. You may fit into one of these descriptions, but whatever your experience you will have one thing in common with all Christians; you will know that Jesus Christ has done something wonderful for you and in you.

Jesus described this to a Jew called Nicodemus as being 'born again' (John 3:3 – see Week 2, study 1 on page 36), that is, experiencing the birth and beginning of a spiritual life in us; before that time we were dead to God.

So what are some of the marks of this new life?

If anyone is in Christ, he is a new creation; the old has gone, the new has come!

2 Corinthians 5: 17

A new friendship

When meeting someone for the first time a variety of questions may come buzzing to mind: 'What will he/she be like?'; 'Will we have anything in common?';

'What will he/she think about this or that?'; 'Will we get on together?' Even after an initial introduction some of these questions remain unanswered. Getting to know people – at least, getting to know them deeply – is a lengthy process. The best friendships take years, even lifetimes, to begin, develop and deepen.

The Bible describes Christians as those who have come to 'know God – or rather are known by God' (Galatians 4: 9). Moses, in the Old Testament, was known as 'the friend of God', and if you have put your trust in God you have begun the most special friendship in your life. It will take a lifetime to develop and deepen. It is not a friendship of equals. Most people want a controllable 'God' in their lives. But a Christian knows that God is the Controller of his life with first place in his thoughts, attitudes and decisions, as Saviour and Lord.

A new forgiveness

You are likely to have discovered that you did not become perfect when you became a Christian! In fact, in this lifetime you never will be. God hates all sin, and the greatest wonder of salvation is that he forgives us. This means that when you trusted in Jesus' death for you, instead of a sentence of 'guilty' you now have 'pardoned' written across the account of your sins – sins past, present and future.

We still live in a sinful world, and what happens when you find yourself sinning yet again? Will God forgive you this time? The answer is yes. God is full of compassion. This does not mean a licence for doing whatever you want, knowing that God will forgive you in the end. (We shall look more closely at God's forgiveness next week.) What God has done for you, your love for him and longing to serve him will mean that you want to stop doing things that displease him. But when you do go wrong, always come back to ask his forgiveness. Keep short accounts with God. Perhaps at night try making a habit of reviewing the past day honestly, asking God's forgiveness and strength to do better.

A new communication

Any friendship can sour, stagnate or start to fizzle out if there is not continually good communication. The same applies to your relationship with God. So how can you make sure that the lines of communication are open?

It is important to spend time with God. Prayer is not merely something recited from a book, although these can be helpful at times. Prayer is rather the baring of innermost thoughts, hopes, problems and aspirations before God who listens. It is being real and honest with him, and finding that he answers.

In Week Six, we shall explore the meaning of prayer more deeply.

A new book

How does God speak? What is he like? What sort of things will please him and enrich your relationship? What has he done for you? The Bible is your source book for these things. It is unique. There is no other book like it, as it is the only book which God himself has directly inspired. It is God's own words, written by men centuries ago, and yet remarkably relevant today, and you will continually be amazed at its truth, not only about God, but about yourself too. More about this next week!

A new enemy

Many people think of the devil as a rather laughable comic character with horns and a forked tail. This is far from the truth. As God is personal, so there is a real, personal devil also. He is not merely some vague, abstract force of opposition, but is actively working for evil and probably all the more as he knows you have now given your life to Jesus Christ. Don't worry – God is stronger, but the Christian life is a fight, so be alert to temptations to sin and resist them.

A new family

Not only are you a child of God when you become a Christian, but you are also a member of the wider Christian family and you are unique in that family, not a clone of other Christians you meet. But there is a new sense of belonging, and you will find that you have the most important things in common with brothers and sisters in Christ regardless of background, race, colour or culture. The church is the expression of the great unity and diversity of the Christian life.

A new responsibility

One of the reasons why all Christians are not immediately whisked away to heaven is that there is a job to do. The majority of the world still does not believe in Jesus and many have never even heard of him. As a Christian you are like an ambassador, not for an earthly king or country, but to speak on behalf of God to others and to tell them of his wonderful message of good news. As we have seen, that's what the word 'gospel' means in Greek: the 'good news' about Jesus Christ.

That does not mean that you have to become a Bible basher or a Billy Graham! We shall look at the Samaritan woman in John's Gospel next week. What an ambassador she was! Jesus had revolutionized her life and it was her instinctive reaction to go and tell others about this Messiah. John 4: 39 says that, 'Many of the Samaritans from that town believed in him because of the woman's testimony.' Evangelism – sharing the good news about Jesus Christ – will be your instinctive reaction to what God has done for you. Tell others, even if it is only a few sentences like the Samaritan woman. Don't worry if you cannot answer all their questions – God will honour and use what you *can* say.

CONVERSATIONS WITH JESUS

Character studies

D o you look at other Christians with dismay, to think that as a Christian you will have to be like them? Or do you slavishly try to copy a Christian in your church or Christian group, without much success, and that leads to despair? Either attitude can be disastrous! Yet we *can* learn so much from watching other Christians who are in touch with God and seeing what God means to them. Don't forget, of course, that we *are* all different yet part of God's same family.

Looking at characters in the Bible is similarly an invaluable way to learn about God. That is what we shall be doing this week – meeting some of the people who talked with Jesus. They were all different from each other and from us, yet they all mattered to Jesus. He showed each of them a little part of both his own character and their own. That is our intention this week – to discover Jesus and learn about ourselves and his plan for our lives.

1. Nicodemus – a religious leader

John 3: 1-15; 7: 45-52; 19: 38-42

The word 'Pharisee' today tends to mean
'hypocritical'. But the original Pharisees were not
necessarily hypocrites; rather they were highly-
principled religious leaders. They certainly held a
position of importance in society.

Nicodemus, who was a Pharisee, came to see Jesus
at night. This may have been because he didn't want
to be seen with Jesus but more likely it was because
it was at night that religious leaders met to debate.
As we read last week, it seems probable from the last
verses of chapter two and the tone of the
conversation, that Nicodemus had already heard
Jesus speak, claiming an authority which the Jewish
leaders didn't like. He would also have seen Jesus'
miraculous signs, or at least have heard about them.
This may partially have awakened his faith. Glance
through the last verses of chapter two of John's
Gospel to refresh your memory of the reactions to
Jesus.

1. *Read John 3: 1-15. Nicodemus asks basically three
questions – verses 2, 4, 9. What wrong ideas lay
behind these questions? Did Nicodemus really think
and behave as though Jesus had come from God?*

_____

_____

_____

_____

_____

36

2. *It is not easy to explain simply what were Jesus'
replies to Nicodemus. But try to put them into your
own words. What important things was Jesus saying
about being a child of God/being part of God's
kingdom? How important are these things to you?*

_____

_____

_____

_____

_____

Note: In verse 5 Jesus speaks of water and the Spirit.
This could be referring to human birth, or to the Old
Testament where water is sometimes connected
with the cleansing which accompanies the work of
the Spirit. Or Jesus may have been talking about the
water of baptism which was associated with
repentance.

3. *Nicodemus' faith in Jesus seemed at the start to be
ill-founded. But he was later prepared to be more
outspoken in Jesus' favour. Read John 7: 45-52. What
extra details do these verses add to the picture you
are building up of Nicodemus?*

_____

_____

_____

_____

_____

_____

4. *The final mention of Nicodemus is in John 19: 38-42. Read these verses and compare the Nicodemus here with the Nicodemus we first met in chapter 3. How has he developed?*

_____

_____

_____

_____

_____

How great is your desire to develop as a Christian – to know Jesus better, to speak out for him and to act for him? Pray that God will give you an increasing desire to grow spiritually.

2. The woman with many husbands

John 4: 1-42

Jesus had time for everyone. One day he might talk with a leading Jewish official, the next, it might be a social outcast. Today we see him talking with a woman (which in itself was socially unacceptable for a man). She was also a Samaritan (that is, a member of the group of people who lived in North Palestine, who had some Jewish blood in them and religious beliefs but in a corrupted and scorned form). Even worse, she was a woman of loose moral behaviour.

1. *Read John 4: 1-42, noting down all we are told about this woman but also observing the gentle way Jesus approached her.*

_____

_____

_____

_____

_____

_____

Try to trace how the woman's understanding of Jesus grew, *e.g.* initially she saw him as no more than a Jewish man who asked her to do an odd thing. Look at verses 9, 11, 12, 15, 19, 20, 25, 29.

2. *How did she react to Jesus? Do you have a similar reaction?*

_____

_____

_____

_____

_____

You may not have seen it this way before, but when you became a Christian you did in fact ask Jesus to give you living water. This living water is both an understanding of the truths about God which cannot be had by those who are strangers to him, and also the Spirit himself who comes to live in the life of the believer.

3. *Spend time thinking about what it means that God has put part of himself, his Spirit, in you and is helping you to understand God himself.*

The corrupted worship of the Samaritans and the worship by the Jews in Jerusalem were both to be replaced by a true worship of the Father (verse 23) which is only possible for those in whom the Spirit lives. Look up Romans 8: 15-16 to see how this can be.

Tell God your Father what it means to you to be his son or daughter – in other words, take time to worship him in Spirit and in truth.

3. The woman who has committed adultery

John 8: 1-11

Once more Jesus is brought face to face with a woman of ill-repute. The Jewish religious leaders wanted to trap Jesus into saying something against either the Roman or Jewish law. They had no compassion. The woman was a pawn in their schemes.

1. *Read John 8: 1-11, contrasting the attitude of Jesus to the woman and the religious leaders' view of her. What difference does Jesus draw between the woman herself and her life of sin? What role does the woman play in this drama?*

_____

_____

_____

_____

_____

Jesus was certainly in a position to pass judgment on sin for he himself had not sinned. Later in this chapter, in disputing with the Jews, he spoke in contrast to them. Look up John 8: 42-47, especially verse 46.

2. *Earlier in his Gospel John clearly explains Jesus' role in coming to judge the world. Turn back to chapter 3: 16-21. What was Jesus' attitude to sin in the world?*

_____

_____

_____

_____

_____

3. *You may wonder if you are just too bad to be accepted by God. How could these verses we have looked at today help you? Or you may be reluctant to turn your back on some habit or attitude which you know is unacceptable to God. What has Jesus said to you today? How might this habit prevent you from coming fully into the light (3: 21)?*

_____

_____

_____

_____

_____

If we tell God we are sorry then he makes us clean. What is more, he forgets about our sin so that we can walk in the light without any sense of shame. Turn to John's first letter in 1 John 1: 5-10. What happens when we confess our sin? What are the effects of walking in the light? Make this into a prayer for yourself today.

4. A blind beggar

John 9: 1-41

You may have already noticed that John writes a great deal about light and darkness. In this story we can read more about this as well as physical and spiritual blindness. This is another beautiful story of Jesus caring for a blind outcast.

1. *Read John 9: 1-41, writing down the stages in which the physical and spiritual blindness of the beggar was gradually dispelled. Contrast this with the blindness of the Pharisees.*

_____

_____

_____

_____

_____

_____

2. *What objections were raised against Jesus and the blind man? See verses 8, 9, 16, 18, 19, 24, 26, 28, 29, 34. What lay at the root of these objections?*

_____

_____

_____

_____

_____

3. *You may encounter many who cross-question you about your Christian faith or even insult you. This could be among friends, family, at work – it can be a very lonely experience, as it was for this man. It is not easy to be a disciple of Jesus. What encouragement can you find in these verses?*

_____

_____

_____

_____

_____

_____

Pause to pray that you will be wise and courageous in speaking out for Jesus and in following him.

Note: Jesus called himself 'Son of Man', a term he frequently used to describe himself. Its origin is in Daniel 7 where it has associations with judgment and authority – which may be why, in the light of the theme of verses 39-41, Jesus used it here.

'Once I was blind, now I can see.' Think back to the time when you were blind to God and, maybe like the Pharisees, were bitterly opposed to him. Thank God that all that has now changed since you are no longer blind. Let verse 38 be your prayer.

5. Jesus' friends in trouble

John 11: 1-46

Like any normal person, Jesus had friends, and in this story his friends in Bethany were in deep distress.

1. *Read John 11: 1-46 and note down all that John tells us about Mary, Martha and Lazarus. What was their friendship with Jesus like? What were the limits of their faith in him?*

_____

_____

_____

_____

_____

_____

2. *Jesus surpassed their expectations. What effects did this have on those present? How could Jesus' actions have helped Martha to understand the conversation she had with Jesus in verses 21-27?*

_____

_____

_____

_____

_____

_____

3. *Jesus was not saying that anyone who believes in him will never die physically, for he himself died. But he was talking about spiritual life which begins now and goes on forever. Try to put verse 25 into your own words. (Remember that Jesus talked about eternal life to the woman at the well in John 4: 14.)*

_____

_____

_____

_____

_____

This Jesus who overcame death and gives life is alive today. How expectant are you that he will answer prayer and do what seems impossible? (Sometimes what we want is not good for us so he does not act and answer as we would choose. We explore the theme of prayer more in Week 6.)

What particular matters are you asking God for? For someone in your family to become a Christian? Or to get more involved in your church? Or guidance for the future? Reassess your prayer requests, then pray with greater confidence in the light of what we have read today.

You may have been struck by Jesus' compassion for his friends. He has a similar love for you. Reflect on how that should affect your daily life and attitudes to God and to others.

Weekend

Read John chapters 6-11 over this weekend.

Memory verse: 'For God so loved the world that he gave his one and only Son, that whoever believes in him shall not perish but have eternal life' (John 3: 16).

The Bible: a bestseller

The Bible has been, and still is, the world's bestseller. At the time of writing, the Bible, in its entirety, has been translated into over 300 languages and over 1,850 languages have at least some portion of it. It is known as one of the most outstanding literary works and it has influenced millions of people. Why? What makes this book so unique and why do Christians want to put into practice what it says? Christians believe two things about the Bible which make it *the* book to live by.

1. The Bible is God's own words, revealed to us

Next time you're with a group of people try and guess what the silent person near you is thinking. You can hazard a guess, but it is impossible to know for sure. In fact you cannot know his intentions or thoughts unless he chooses to reveal them and let you know. This is what words and actions do – they communicate our thoughts. It would also be impossible to understand God's mind and intentions unless he had somehow made them knowable. He has done this in two major ways. Firstly, through Christ. John calls him the 'Word' at the beginning of his Gospel. And words communicate. So Christ is God's living Word of communication to us, to tell us who he is, as we saw in Week 1. Secondly, God has chosen the written words of the Bible to tell us his mind on certain things. He has actually spoken to us, and as we use words to speak, so God has also used words. The apostle Paul describes it as:

> *All Scripture is God-breathed and is useful for teaching, rebuking, correcting and training in righteousness, so that the man of God may be thoroughly equipped for every good work.*

2 Timothy 3:16-17

2. The Bible is man's own words, used by God

God did not use people as dictating machines to take down his messages, neither did they hear voices from heaven. But, by the Holy Spirit, God spoke *through* the writers. So there are different types of literature in the Bible, reflecting the different characters and personalities of the men who wrote them. There are the Old Testament writers who chronicled historical facts; King David who poured out his heart in the Psalms; the prophet Amos who was a shepherd; the contemplative apostle John whose Gospel is more reflective than the other three Gospels; and many more. God did not bypass the people or their personalities, but worked through them.

So the Bible is unique because it is both truly human and truly divine.

> *The double authorship of the Bible will affect the way in which we read it. Because it is the*

word of men, we shall study it like every other book, using our minds, investigating its words and syntax, its historical origin and its literary composition. But because it is also the Word of God, we shall study it like no other book, on our knees, humbly, crying to God for illumination and for the ministry of the Holy Spirit, without whom we can never understand his Word.

John Stott,
The Bible: Book for Today (IVP)

The message of the Bible

The Bible is all about God and it is all about people – you. The two belong together and this is the book that tells us how. No other book can tell us the truth about God: his character, his creation and his plan of how to deal with the mess humanity has made. Jesus once said to some Jews, 'You diligently study the Scriptures [they would have had the Old Testament] because you think that by them you possess eternal life. These are the Scriptures that testify about me ...' (John 5: 39). So it should not surprise us that Jesus Christ is the pivotal theme in the whole of the Bible. The Old Testament prophesies and looks forward to his coming and the New Testament recounts his coming and the purpose of it: to live and die in order to make a way for human beings to get in touch with God again. John says about his Gospel that he wrote it for a specific purpose:

... that you may believe that Jesus is the Christ, the Son of God, and that by believing you may have life in his name.

John 20: 31

What is the Bible?

The word *biblos* was the common Greek word for any book, from which we derive the word for *the* book, the Bible. Yet really the Bible is not one book but a set of sixty-six separate books collected into one.

Chapter and verse

The Bible was not originally written with chapters and verses, or the headings which you may find in some Bibles between paragraphs or at the top of a page. These have been put in later to make it easier to find our way round. There is a fairly standard way of writing references for passages. For example, 2 Corinthians 5: 17 means the second letter to the Corinthians, chapter 5 and verse 17.

Feeding on the Bible

The Bible is food for thought and action. It may have been written in another time, another culture and by people you have probably never even heard of. But one of the ways in which you will know that it is God's book as well as man's book is that it will speak to you with amazing relevance. God will use the Bible to change your mind and your life to be more like his. It won't happen all in one day – you couldn't cope with that! But it will be gradual and steady.

Being a Christian is living a new life and any new life needs nourishment. Sometimes it may be a feast, sometimes something more ordinary, but the purpose of food is to encourage healthy, proper growth. Feeding on God's word is like that too. You will grow as a Christian through regular Bible study.

The Old Testament was originally written in Hebrew (with Ezra and part of Daniel in Aramaic), and it comprises thirty-nine different books, from Genesis to Malachi.

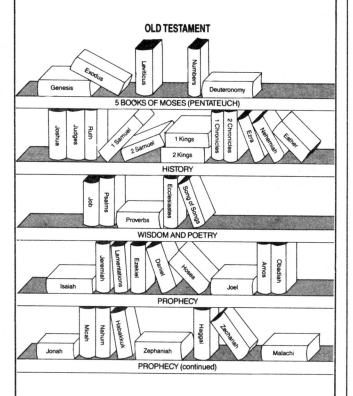

OLD TESTAMENT

Genesis · Exodus · Leviticus · Numbers · Deuteronomy
5 BOOKS OF MOSES (PENTATEUCH)

Joshua · Judges · Ruth · 1 Samuel · 2 Samuel · 1 Kings · 2 Kings · 1 Chronicles · 2 Chronicles · Ezra · Nehemiah · Esther
HISTORY

Job · Psalms · Proverbs · Ecclesiastes · Song of Songs
WISDOM AND POETRY

Isaiah · Jeremiah · Lamentations · Ezekiel · Daniel · Hosea · Joel · Amos · Obadiah
PROPHECY

Jonah · Micah · Nahum · Habakkuk · Zephaniah · Haggai · Zechariah · Malachi
PROPHECY (continued)

It is called the *Old* Testament because it covers a time-span from creation to about 400 years BC, and deals with God's creation and plan for mankind, especially through his chosen people of Israel, and his preparation throughout history for the coming of Christ.

The New Testament was originally written in Greek. It comprises twenty-seven different books, from Matthew's Gospel to Revelation.

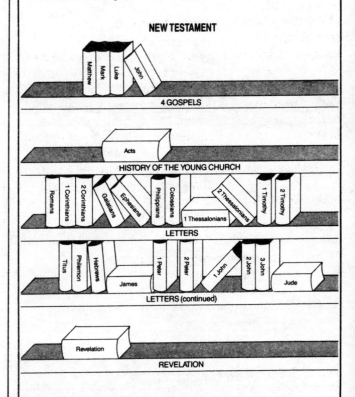

NEW TESTAMENT

4 GOSPELS

Matthew | Mark | Luke | John

HISTORY OF THE YOUNG CHURCH

Acts

LETTERS

Romans | 1 Corinthians | 2 Corinthians | Galatians | Ephesians | Philippians | Colossians | 1 Thessalonians | 2 Thessalonians | 1 Timothy | 2 Timothy

LETTERS (continued)

Titus | Philemon | Hebrews | James | 1 Peter | 2 Peter | 1 John | 2 John | 3 John | Jude

REVELATION

Revelation

This is called the *New* Testament because it deals with the new part of God's plan and purpose for us with the coming of Christ. It covers the historical details of his birth, life, death and resurrection; the expansion of the early church; several important letters to early Christians; and one book of revelation to the apostle John about things that are to come.

You may not always feel like it, but persevere. Biblical food is nourishing and benefiting even if you don't feel like it.

When is the best time to read the Bible?

Find the best time for you, when you are awake and alert, able to find somewhere quiet and undisturbed. This may mean having to set the alarm clock a little earlier than usual. It is certainly better than just before you slip off to sleep, as you won't take much in then. Whenever it is, spend quality time with God. Some Christians call this a 'quiet time': a time for quiet talking with God and paying attention to his word. Pray that he will make it alive to you. It will make all the difference to each day.

STOP!   ACTION!

Take a moment to look ahead to the next week. Make a regular, daily appointment to meet with God.

Where do I start?

Most books begin at the beginning. So does the Bible. You could begin at Genesis and read straight through to Revelation, but you might get bogged down in Leviticus and be tempted to give up. The Bible is a collection of books and it is possible to start in the middle! In this book we have suggested the Gospel of John as a good place to begin. The Old Testament is indispensable, but you will probably find the New Testament a little easier to grasp if you are a beginner.

A modern version of the Bible is a good thing to have. The Authorized Version is a beautiful translation, but difficult to understand at times. Try the New International Version, the Revised Standard Version or the Good News Bible.

Bible study involves effort

The Bible is not a novel or piece of science fiction. It is immediately understandable on one level, but you will have questions and things you don't understand. Studying the Bible involves asking the Holy Spirit to help you, plus some effort and hard work on your part. Keep a note of your questions and discuss them with a more experienced Christian.

THE HOLY SPIRIT

A topic study

In chapters 1, 3 and 4 we have already seen
references to the Spirit. He came upon Jesus at his
baptism; he gives life; he cannot be controlled by
any man; he makes it possible for people to worship
God. But the disciples of Jesus did not understand all
this until Jesus had died, risen again and then gone
back to be with God, his father.

You may, however, be asking, how did the Spirit
come in the first place and what does he do? Who is
he? He has existed since before time. There are many
references to his activity in the Old Testament. We
however shall begin in John's Gospel and then look
at other parts of the New Testament. The answers to
the above questions should come clearer through
this week.

1. The promise of the Spirit

John 7: 37-39; Acts 1: 1-11

1. *Turn to John 7: 37-39. This festival of Tabernacles was an eight-day harvest thanksgiving, thanking God for the harvest and praying for next year's rainfall. The last day marked the climax. From these verses, which of the following statements are true and which are false? Give reasons for your answers.*

(a) Jesus himself was claiming to be in a position to offer the Spirit to others.

_____

_____

(b) The Spirit was given to all people.

_____

_____

(c) The Spirit had been totally silent and inactive up to that time.

_____

_____

(d) Once Jesus had been glorified (or raised to glory), then the Spirit would take his place.

_____

_____

If you answered (c) as true you must have forgotten the study of Jesus' baptism in chapter 1. And the statement in (d) may have puzzled you. So ...

2. *Turn now to Acts 1: 1-11. What teaching is Jesus giving to the disciples about the Holy Spirit? What effects would the Spirit have on those who received him? Why was he given to them?*

_____

_____

_____

_____

_____

_____

_____

Note: The ascension of Jesus into heaven was when he was completely glorified.

3. *Summarize all you have so far discovered about the Holy Spirit. During this week you might like to build up a dossier on him.*

_____

_____

_____

_____

_____

_____

Try to imagine what it would be like if the Spirit had not come in place of Jesus. Turn your thoughts into thanksgiving to God that he gave the Spirit.

2. What does the Spirit do?

John 14 – 16

John gives a lengthy record of the last long
conversation that Jesus had with his disciples; this is
to be found in John chapters 14 – 16 and needs to be
read many times over. We shall be looking today
only at the parts where Jesus takes care to explain
the Holy Spirit's role in the future. He keeps returning
to the subject – an indication of the importance he
places on the Spirit.

1. *Divide the space below into two and then read the
following verses. Note down on one side what Jesus
says about the Spirit's relationship with the Father
and with himself. On the other side write down what
he says the Spirit will do for the disciples and in the
world.*
   John 14: 15-17, 25-26; 15: 26-27; 16: 5-15.

_____

_____

_____

_____

_____

_____

2. *Repeat to yourself in your own words how the
Spirit relates to God the Father and to Jesus, the Son.
Does he ever act independently of them? Why can we
confidently refer to the Holy Spirit as 'he', as a
person?*

_____

_____

_____

_____

Take each of the things which you wrote down in the
second column about the Spirit's role in the life of
the disciples. Pray that you may know him doing
each of these things in your own life.

3. *You may have noticed that the teaching about the
Spirit was surrounding instructions about the
possible suffering of Jesus' disciples, e.g. 15: 18-25.
Why might the Spirit be particularly important to
those who are undergoing persecution or are
misunderstood for their faith?*

_____

_____

_____

_____

4. *Are you praying specifically for someone to
become a Christian? Pray for them in the light of
John 16: 8-11.*

> **[The Spirit's] very presence will be a
> demonstration to the world which condemned
> Jesus that he was in the right and they were in
> the wrong ... [Jesus'] rejection, condemnation
> and execution expressed in violent clarity the
> world's refusal to believe in him ...**

> F.F. Bruce,
> *The Gospel of John* (Pickering)

3. At last … he's here in power

Acts 2:1-47

Jesus has been glorified. He has returned to be with his Father. The disciples have been waiting ten days for something to happen, for the promised gift to come. And now …

1. *Read Acts 2: 1-13, trying.to capture the excitement and dynamism of this historic occasion. What would you pick out as the most significant factors if you were writing a newspaper report?*

_____

_____

_____

_____

_____

2. *How did these events in Acts 2: 1-41 prove that Jesus' teaching about the Spirit was true? As you refer back to the last two studies, note down which verses in Acts 2 refer to the teaching of Jesus in John and Acts 1. For example:*

- *the disciples began to worship God (John 4: 23).*
- *the disciples would have power to speak to people in Jerusalem (Acts 1: 8).*
- *the Spirit was to help people understand Jesus' ministry (John 15: 26-27).*
- *the Spirit was given after Jesus was glorified (John 7: 39).*

_____

_____

_____

_____

_____

Note: Having come in such a dramatic way, the Holy Spirit has never gone away. He has come to transform the lives of all new believers in the same way that he did on the first day of Pentecost. Once begun, that work continues throughout the rest of life.

3. *How did the Spirit affect the everyday living of the early Christians? (Acts 2: 42-47)*

_____

_____

_____

_____

_____

Spend time praying that you may know the confidence and power of the Spirit at work in your own life – both in what you say about Jesus and also in how you actually live your life.

The adopted pattern of life for these early Christians may not necessarily be appropriate for you in every way, but it acts as a challenge to your own lifestyle.

If you are making a dossier on the Holy Spirit, add what else you have found out about him.

4. Living by the Spirit

Romans 8: 1-17; Galatians 5: 16-26

It has become obvious over the last three studies

that the Holy Spirit is in the business of changing lives, helping people to be more like Jesus.

1. *Look up Romans 8: 1-17. As you read these verses make a list of characteristics of someone who is living according to the Spirit, in contrast to someone who is not i.e. those who live according to their human nature. You should find at least four things.*

_____

_____

_____

_____

2. *Turn now to Galatians 5: 16-26. The apostle Paul wrote both these letters to the Roman and Galatian Christians. What does it mean for the Christian to live by the Spirit?*

_____

_____

_____

_____

3. *Some people say you just sit back and let God and his Spirit do everything in your life without any effort on the part of the individual concerned. How do these verses contradict such a view? How can you co-operate with the Spirit?*

_____

_____

_____

_____

_____

Slowly take each aspect of verses 22 and 23 and pray that the fruit of the Spirit will become increasingly evident in your life. Are you committed to ensuring that your prayer is answered?

5. The Spirit gives power to the church

Romans 12: 1-8; 1 Corinthians 12: 1-11; Ephesians 4: 11-13

Birthdays are times for presents. The day of Pentecost, which is sometimes called the birthday of the church, is no exception. God gave lots of gifts to his church that day. He is still giving such presents to his church. That is what we shall be looking at today.

1. *Read Romans 12: 1-8, noting down what gifts God has given to his body, the church. Would you expect one person in the church to possess all these gifts? How are the gifts to be used?*

_____

_____

_____

_____

_____

2. *Turn then to 1 Corinthians 12: 1-11. In the church in Corinth some people seemed to be arguing about which gifts were most important and some were even becoming proud of their gifts. First of all add to your list from Romans what other gifts Paul mentions here. Who gives the gifts? What answer does Paul have for those who are boasting of their gifts?*

_____

_____

63

_____

_____

_____

You have a responsibility to use wisely whatever God has given you. Are you prepared for that?

3. *Finally, turn to Ephesians 4: 11-13 and write down the further gifts of which Paul writes. Why were these gifts given? With what expected results?*

_____

_____

_____

_____

_____

You may be unsure what gifts God has given you. He can give and take away gifts as appropriate and it may not yet be apparent how he is going to use you in his church. Don't get anxious or self-analytical nor compare yourself with others. Just pray that you will be ready and willing to serve God in your local church or further afield. It may be that it will be others who first recognize God's gift to you.

Weekend

We suggest that you read John 12 – 17 over this weekend, which will also help you to review this week's studies.

Memory verse: 'Jesus answered, "I am the way and the truth and the life. No-one comes to the Father except through me"' (John 14: 6).

Meet the Holy Spirit

'Trinity' is not a word you will find in your Bible, but it does express the truth found there that we worship *one* God in *three* persons. The Father, Son and Holy Spirit share an equality in being God as well as a difference in the things that they do. The Holy Spirit, therefore, is not an 'it', but a 'he'. He is personal and his name tells us much about him.

In John chapter 3 Jesus says that the Spirit is like the wind. In fact the Greek word for spirit also means wind. Just as the wind cannot be seen, neither can the Spirit, but it is always possible to recognize where he has been. The Spirit is also 'holy' – set apart from sin and loving everything good and godly.

The Holy Spirit does many things for the believer. In fact it is impossible to be a Christian without his work.

Firstly, in becoming a Christian, the Holy Spirit makes the victory of Christ's death and resurrection real in your life. He is the one who brings about a new spiritual life and nature. He also gives you assurance of your faith (see 1 John 3: 24). If you believe that Christ died for you and things are now right between you and God – that is the Holy Spirit's work, although you may not have realized it!

Secondly, in being a Christian, it is the Holy Spirit who enables you to fulfil God's will. He gives a new power to resist temptation and sin and to serve and love God instead. He 'sanctifies' you. That is, he works with you to make you holy, bringing in moral renewal, a change of character and a new direction toward God. This will not happen in a flash, and it will not be completed on earth, but the Holy Spirit's aim is to make you more and more like Christ. That does not mean effortless perfection. He will not do it without your co-operation.

As an apple tree bears fruit, so there will be Christian fruit to be seen in the life of the believer (have a look at Galatians 5: 16). The famous passage of 1 Corinthians 13 particularly shows that *love* is the crowning proof of the Spirit's presence, both individually and together as Christians.

Can't I be a Christian without going to church?

The answer is yes and no! Yes, of course it is possible to be a Christian without going to church. Christianity is a matter of faith, not observed ritual, and going to church does not *make* a person a Christian any more than a weekly visit to an airport would make him a plane! The primary evidence of Christians is not that they go to church, but that they know and love Christ. It is all about a Person, not a place. It is unfortunate that the same English word, *church*, is used to cover both a building and the body of believers. The church is really all about the people, not the place.

Going to church is not necessary for salvation, but it is necessary for growth. Some people's 'faith' seems to be so private that they hardly seem to know it themselves and it is scarcely apparent to anyone else.

Christians have always, where humanly possible, met together and for good reasons. They *want* to meet together to learn more about God, to grow, to

66

encourage one another and to be a stronger, more effective witness to the world than would be possible alone. Jesus' promise is that 'where two or three come together in my name, there am I with them' (Matthew 18:20). God meets with his people in a special way when they are together. You may find that you do not like all the members of this body of believers, or naturally get on with them. Jesus welcomed the outcasts as well as the rich, fishermen and tax collectors, the uneducated and the brilliant. Your church will be a mixture of all sorts, but they are your brothers and sisters. Together you will love, serve, respect and encourage one another. You are committed to them and they to you.

The church is also wider than the local church to which you belong; it stretches throughout the world and over all time. God's aim is for *the whole world* to hear about him; and God's church is a missionary church. Every Christian has an international responsibility. Some actually *go* to another country to pass on the good news, but all Christians *pray* for and *support* the church worldwide.

Choosing a church

The beauty of the building or its architecture is really irrelevant! Find a church which is:

- committed to teaching and obeying God's word.
- a group of people showing God's love in action.

THINKING ABOUT JESUS

John 13 – A meditation

Questions, questions and more questions. You may be someone who is naturally inquisitive, always wanting to know more. That is a great ability to use as you study the Bible. Or you may be someone who is an activist – always on the move. In serving God, that is indispensable. Yet you may be so busy mentally or physically that you never find time to be still and quiet in God's presence, just enjoying his company and meditating on his words to us.

We are going to spend this week reflecting upon John 13. We may be asking lots of questions to stimulate reflection, but mainly we shall be drawing out themes for thought. Take time and just relax. God is with you and wants to speak to you. Listen to him.

A thought on the seashore

*In ev'ry object here I see
Something, O Lord, that leads to thee;
Firm as the rocks thy promise stands,
Thy mercies countless as the sands,
Thy love a sea immensely wide,
Thy grace an ever-flowing tide.*

*In ev'ry object here I see
Something, my heart, that points at thee:
Hard as the rocks that bound the strand,
Unfruitful as the barren sand,
Deep and deceitful as the ocean,
And, like the tides, in constant motion.*

John Newton (1725-1807)

1. Jesus: with a purpose

God my Father, the timetable of my life is overloaded. My mind seems crammed with the responsibilities and decisions of this day. But as you are never too busy for me, help me to have time for you. Quieten my thoughts, let me relax in your presence, let me enjoy being with you. I ask this through Jesus Christ himself. Amen.

1. *Slowly read through John 13. As you do so, look out for signs of these two attitudes of Jesus:*

■ *Jesus knew that his life had a purpose. It was not wheeling out of his control.*

_____

_____

_____

_____

■ *Jesus had a unique relationship with God his Father.*

_____

_____

_____

2. *After the crucifixion, some people may have thought Jesus' life had been wasted. The resurrection soon scotched that idea. Try to put into your own words why it is important to you that Jesus' life (and death) had a purpose.*

_____

_____

_____

_____

_____

3. *Your own life cannot have the same significance as Jesus' life. At times you may wonder how important you are. As a Christian, what is your purpose in living? You might like to look up Romans 8: 28-30 to give you some ideas.*

_____

_____

_____

_____

_____

Jesus' relationship with his Father was indeed unique, yet he gave up all the glory and security of heaven to come to this earth. Take time to thank God that Jesus was willing to do this for us. Reading Philippians 2: 5-11 would help to direct your thoughts.

2. Jesus: what were his rights?

Thy life was given for me
What have I given to thee?

Lord Jesus, right now I want to give you my thoughts and my time. Help me to concentrate upon you. For your sake. Amen.

'Fight for your rights.'

'That's not fair!'

In our world we expect to have to stand up for our rights at any cost. Down the centuries Christians have championed the cause of those deprived of basic rights of life – for example, for freedom from fear, injustice or poverty. But what about our own status and supposed rights?

1. *Slowly read the first seventeen verses of John 13, trying to understand Jesus' attitude to his rights and status. Why did he behave as he did?*

_____

_____

_____

_____

72

2. *What status or prominent position do you hold? How do you want others to view you? How prepared are you to undertake menial tasks in order to serve others? What expectations do you have of how others should treat and respect you?*

_____

_____

_____

_____

_____

3. *Reflect on the various relationships you have with friends, family, colleagues or neighbours. In what ways can you take Christ's example and act on it? You will no doubt need to ask for God's help.*

_____

_____

_____

_____

_____

O Lord, our Christ, may we have thy mind and thy spirit; make us instruments of thy peace; where there is hatred, let us sow love; where there is injury, pardon; where there is discord, union; where there is doubt, faith; where there is despair, hope; where there is darkness, light; and where there is sadness, joy.

O divine Master, grant that we may not so much seek to be consoled as to console; to be understood, as to understand; to be loved, as to love; for it is in giving that we receive; it is in

pardoning that we are pardoned; and it is in
dying that we are born to eternal life. Amen.

Prayer of Francis of Assisi (*c.*1182-1226)

3. Jesus: betrayed

Holy Spirit, fill me with your presence and peace.
Indeed, fill me so much that all distractions will be
gone and I can concentrate every part of myself upon
God. Amen.

Have you ever experienced the pain of being let
down by a friend whom you trusted? If so, try to
recall your emotional reactions at the time. If not, try
to imagine what it must be like.

1. *Briefly read through John 13: 1-17, reminding
yourself of how Jesus had already demonstrated his
love for Judas.*

2. *More slowly read verses 18-30. Despite the
knowledge he had of Judas, how did Jesus react to
him? What lesson was Jesus teaching about how his
followers should react to those opposed to them?
What about yourself?*

_____

_____

_____

_____

_____

Note: For a host to offer a guest a particularly
appetizing morsel at a feast was to single out that
guest as a special friend.

The Lord himself states that the Scripture had to be fulfilled in Judas' action. This does not mean that Judas in particular was driven to his act of treachery by a decree of fate against which it would have been fruitless to struggle. Even if Jesus' betrayal by one of his intimate companions was foreseen, it was by Judas' personal choice that he, rather than anyone else, eventually filled that role.

F.F. Bruce,
The Gospel of John (Pickering)

3. *Jesus knew the thoughts in Judas' mind although Judas wouldn't have thanked him for it. Since becoming a Christian you may have discovered that God knows you through and through – nothing is hidden. This could unnerve you or could cause you to be grateful. The psalmist expresses this very clearly in Psalm 139. Read that psalm, turning lines from it into your own personal prayer to God (for example, verses 23, 24).*

_____

_____

_____

_____

_____

_____

4. *Turning his back on Jesus, Judas went out into the night. It was dark outside, but also dark inside his soul. Until recently you too may have known nothing of the light of Jesus inside your life. Pray for any you know who are still in the dark.*

4. Jesus: shows what love means

Help me to 'practise the presence of God'.

Brother Lawrence

What happens if a mother finds she cannot love her child; or love has died in a marriage; or two colleagues at work hate the sight of each other; or two members of a church cannot get on together? Try once more and then give up? What answer would you give in each situation?

1. *Turn to John 13: 34-35. Read these verses through several times. Jesus' instructions may sound so simple, yet to obey them is no easy task. Take each phrase and think over what Jesus is saying. How did he show that it is possible to put this into practice? You may find it helps to imagine that you are explaining Jesus' words to someone who knows little about Jesus but wants to know more.*

_____

_____

_____

_____

_____

_____

_____

2. *What are the effects of such behaviour? (Remember this is a specific command for Christians in relating to one another.) Are there people you find it hard to love truly, in the way that Jesus did? How*

much is loving an act of the will rather than an
unreliable emotion? What are you going to do about
these people you find hard to love? Do they have to
love you in return?

_____

_____

_____

_____

_____

Turn your thoughts into prayer.
  John records other occasions when Jesus
commands his disciples to love one another. Turn to
John 15: 9-17 for one example.

3. *In the first century it was said of the early church,*
'See how these Christians love one another.' How
determined are you that this should be said of you
and of your church fellowship or Christian group?

_____

_____

_____

5. Jesus with his disciples

Let me have my way among you,
Do not strive, do not strive.

Graham Kendrick

Father, I know this is what you want for me. May it be

true in my life today – both right now and forever.
Amen.

John 13 shows us Jesus with his chosen disciples.
Today we are going to look at one of these men,
Peter, always in the front row of any portrait of the
disciples! He occurs in three incidents in this chapter
alone.

1. *Read the chapter through and note down what
John tells us about Peter. What sort of man was he?
How did he relate to Jesus? What do you think he
expected being a disciple of Jesus was like?*

_____

_____

_____

_____

_____

_____

2. *Are there ways in which you are like him? For
instance, do you hate being dependent upon others?
Do you always want to know what is going on? Do
you make rash promises you cannot keep?*

_____

_____

_____

_____

_____

_____

3. *Note how Jesus handled Peter. Spend time reflecting on how willing you are to let Jesus touch your weak points, in order that you will 'bear fruit for God' (to quote John in chapter 15). Pray about your willingness.*

When you realized you had committed your life to Jesus, had you seriously considered what it might cost? Peter thought he had, but when the test came, he failed, as Jesus predicted in verse 38. Think over what it has already cost you to be disciple – and also how prepared you are to give everything to God.

_____

_____

_____

_____

Weekend

Over this weekend, read John 18 – 21. It will prepare you for next week's studies.

Memory verse: 'A new command I give you: Love one another. As I have loved you, so you must love one another' (John 13:34).

Discipleship and spiritual warfare

Daring to be disciples

We all know about the twelve disciples. They were men whom Jesus specially chose to be with him during his most important three years of earthly ministry. They were an unusual bunch, ranging from fishermen to a tax collector! But they were called *disciples* for a good reason. The word means someone with 'L' plates on – a learner. They were learners of Jesus.

You are also called to be a disciple today. It may not be easy to follow Jesus. You may find yourself swimming against the tide, being 'different' from your friends in the way you think about God and the life you live. It may bring scorn or ridicule from others at home or at work. Perhaps you have found that you seem to have more problems now than when you had your back turned on God! If everything in the Christian garden is not rosy, does that mean that there's no point in following Christ? No. There are good reasons for this. Don't think that you are unique. Peter says in his letter, 'To this you were called, because Christ suffered for you, leaving you an example, that you should follow in his steps' (1 Peter 2: 21).

Soldiers

Becoming a Christian is not a matter of swallowing a sugar-coated pill to protect you from danger and harm. Christians do not float six feet above troubles! The Bible uses the metaphor of being a soldier, enlisting for battle and learning to overcome the traps, temptations, sorrows and scars of the fight. It is not a holiday camp, but a training ground.

> *... In saying, 'Count the cost,' what am I saying? Am I suggesting that it is possible to live as a Christian without warfare? For this is not true. The real counting should have been done before you became a Christian.* To acknowledge Jesus as Saviour and Lord is to join an army. Whether you know it or not, you have enlisted. *The only other option open to you is to become a deserter, to hide your uniform and pretend you are someone whom you are not. Now to be a deserter is not to* leave *the army (celestial regulations make no provision for the discharge of personnel) but to evade your responsibility to your commanding officer.*
>
> John White, *The Fight* (IVP)

The battle is, as the old puritans used to put it, against the world, the flesh and the devil.

The world – against desires which become gods for us; goals ousting God out of the first place in our affections. The Bible calls us to be *in* the world, but not of it.

The flesh – against those things which our 'old' self would tend to want and to do; the old habits and sins and tendencies to do even the very opposite of what we know Christ really wants.

The devil – against all the ways in which the devil

will use you to hinder the cause of Christ. He will accuse you, tempt you, make you despair and try to ruin you. He is your fiendish enemy. Don't underestimate him. At the same time, don't live in continual fear of him – he has been overcome through Christ's death and resurrection. Jesus *is* Lord ... in your life as well!

Being a disciple is taking seriously that Jesus is not only *Saviour* but also *Lord* in your life, right from the start. The saying goes, 'He's either Lord of all or he's not Lord at all.' He has set you free from sin by dying for you as your Saviour. Freedom is a thing to be greatly prized. But it would be ludicrous to imagine a train wanting to break free of the rails and go it alone. To be truly free, the train needs to move easily along those rails and to do what it was made for. Christ has set you free *from* sin and free *to do* what is right and what you were made for; to live under his Lordship day by day out of gratitude for all he has done.

When ... it comes to reaching the world for Christ, or producing a man of God, there are no short cuts .... So many Christians act as though they were on a conveyor belt to heaven at the least possible cost. Yet God did not create us to live this life at a minimum cost. What was his purpose? Not just that we should be saved and thus get back to where we ought to have started, but rather that we should go on to conquest and worship and joy and life in abundance.

George Verwer,
No Turning Back (Hodder and STL)

THE CROSS

John 18–21 – A bird's-eye view

The aim of this type of study is to read through
fairly long passages to get an overall grasp of their
contents and the events they portray. That may
mean skipping over some of the detail, but when you
go back to look at that later it will make more sense if
you know what the passage as a whole is about. If
you read these chapters over the weekend the
passages will already be slightly familiar to you.

Chapters 18 – 21 form the climax of John's Gospel.
Events had been leading up to Jesus' death and
resurrection from a long way back in the narrative.
The Jewish authorities' hostility to Jesus' teaching
had been building up, until eventually they plotted
his death (John 11: 45-57); but more importantly,
Jesus himself had been looking towards the cross as
the culmination of his earthly ministry throughout
his public teaching (e.g. John 3: 14-15; 10: 11; 13: 1).
A large part of the chapter we looked at last week is
taken up with Jesus' preparation of his disciples for
what is about to happen – and Peter has responded
by promising to stand by Jesus, whatever the cost
(John 13: 37).

1. Arrested

John 18: 1-27

Read through the passage and try to imagine how
Peter must have felt as these events unfolded.

1. *Why do you think Peter attacked Malchus (verse
10)?*

_____

_____

2. *After this show of bravery, why did Peter then
deny he was a follower of Jesus (verses 17, 25, 27)?*

_____

_____

3. *Can you think of situations where you would
prefer people not to know you are a Christian? Or
where you find it hard to say you are a Christian?*

_____

_____

Are there any people you know who don't realize
you're a follower of Jesus? If so, pray for the right
opportunities (and the courage!) to tell them.

4. *You will remember what you read about Peter last
week. You might describe him as impulsive and
inconsistent in his actions here. How would you
describe Jesus' reactions to the events in this
passage?*

_____

_____

_____

_____

_____

Notes: 18: 3 The band of soldiers could have been as many as 600 men. 18: 5 'I am' was the Jewish name for God (Exodus 3: 14) – see page 16. Jesus' use of it could have startled the crowd (verse 6). 18: 20–21 Jesus refused to answer questions himself because in Jewish law a prisoner could only be convicted by witnesses.

2. He suffered under Pontius Pilate

John 18: 28 – 19: 16

Although Jesus' trial before the High Priest did not result in any definite accusations, the Jews took him to Pilate for sentencing. It is ironic that they should be concerned about ritual uncleanness (18: 28) while plotting such a flagrant miscarriage of justice.

1. *Make a list of the reasons the Jews gave to Pilate for having Jesus executed.*

_____

_____

_____

_____

_____

2. *What sort of man do you think Pilate thought Jesus was?*

_____

_____

_____

3. *What were his motives in finally agreeing to Jesus' execution?*

_____

_____

_____

_____

_____

In John 19:11, Jesus recognizes that even these dreadful events are within God's control. Look up Romans 8:28 and write it out below (it is a good verse to learn!).

_____

_____

_____

_____

_____

_____

4. *Can you think of ways in which this verse is true for Jesus in these events of his trial, death and resurrection?*

_____

_____

_____

_____

_____

5. *Can you think of any times in your own life when God has brought something good out of apparent disaster?*

_____

_____

_____

_____

As you come to pray, thank God for the times he's looked after you in the past and pray for any difficult situations you face now in the light of Romans 8: 28.

Notes: 18: 28 See Exodus 12: 18–19 – there would be yeast in a Gentile's house. 18: 32 See Leviticus 24: 16 – Jewish law prescribed execution by stoning.

3. Crucified, dead and buried

John 19: 17-42

Read this account of Jesus' death on the cross. As you do so, your first response should be one of worship and thankfulness that Jesus should willingly go through all this for us. Before you go any further with this study, stop and thank God for sending Jesus to die for us – you may like to use this hymn:

When I survey the wondrous cross,
On which the Prince of Glory died,
My richest gain I count but loss,
And pour contempt on all my pride.

See from His head, His hands, His feet,
Sorrow and love flow mingled down;
Did e'er such love and sorrow meet,
Or thorns compose so rich a crown?

Isaac Watts (1674-1748)

In his account, John draws out the way Jesus' death fulfilled the Old Testament Scriptures; you may like to look up some of the following references if you have time:

■ verse 24 quotes Psalm 22: 18
■ verse 28 is more difficult to identify – perhaps Psalm 69: 21, or Psalm 42: 2
■ verse 36 – see Exodus 12: 46; Numbers 9: 12 – both these passages refer to the Passover lamb, which was killed to protect the Israelites as they left Egypt (you can read about it in the rest of Exodus 12). This was a role John the Baptist foretold for Jesus (John 1: 29). This verse also refers to Psalm 34: 20
■ verse 37 quotes Zechariah 12: 10

1. *What point do you think John is making by emphasizing ways in which Jesus' death fulfilled the Old Testament Scriptures?*

_____

_____

_____

_____

Notes: When Jesus cried, 'It is finished' (verse 30), it was with a sense of accomplishment, not resignation, as all through his ministry he had seen his death as part of his God-given job on earth (*e.g.* John 3:14-15; 10: 11; 12: 32-33; 14: 2-3), something he had to do for those who followed him.

4. On the third day ...

John 20

Did Jesus really rise from the dead? Couldn't the early church have made up the whole story? To what conclusion does the evidence point? How important is it anyway?

As you might expect, the resurrection of Christ continues to be a matter of debate. If you want to examine the evidence more fully, try reading *Who moved the stone?* by Frank Morison (STL) – a classic book, written by someone who set out to disprove Christianity by showing that the resurrection couldn't possibly have happened, but ended up utterly convinced that it had. Also worth reading, and briefer is *The Evidence for the Resurrection* by Norman Anderson (IVP booklet).

1. *Look at the reactions of three individuals in this chapter. What was it that convinced John (the 'other disciple' in verse 2), Mary Magdalene and Thomas that Jesus really had been dead?*

_____

_____

Note: Verse 7: This is the position the grave-clothes would have been in when wrapped around Jesus' body – they hadn't been unwound!

2. *Jesus was patient with Thomas' doubts. What help can you find here for someone today who finds it hard to accept the truth of the resurrection?*

_____

_____

_____

_____

_____

One result of the resurrection was that Jesus gave his disciples the Spirit he had promised (verse 22; John 16: 7), and with him a commission to preach the good news of forgiveness and new life (verse 23).

3. *Look through the chapter again – what other differences did it make to the people Jesus met when they realized he really had been raised?*

_____

_____

_____

_____

_____

4. *What are the differences it makes to your faith and lifestyle to believe that Jesus has risen?*

_____

_____

_____

_____

5. Ransomed, healed, restored, forgiven ...

John 21

1. *Why might the disciples have gone back to their old work? Do you think they were right to do so?*

_____

_____

_____

_____

2. *Why do you think Jesus asked Peter three times about his love for him? (Heavy hint: most commentators see a link between this chapter and the events of chapter 18!)*

_____

_____

_____

_____

_____

3. *Can you think of times when you've let Jesus down? Stop and ask his forgiveness for them now. It's something we all do (look up 1 John 1: 8-9 to encourage you), but it doesn't mean Jesus has no further use for you – he still had plans for Peter.*

4. *Jesus repeats his call to Peter, 'Follow me' (verse 19). What does this passage say that will involve for Peter?*

Note: Verse 22 suggests that Jesus had different plans for John – and his service for Jesus did turn out to be different from Peter's. Tradition says that Peter died as a martyr in Rome (see verses 18-19), while John lived to a ripe old age and had the task of making sure people knew what Jesus was really like, long after the events of his life, death and resurrection (as in this Gospel and his Letters).

Jesus has a plan for your life too, though he may not tell you much about it yet. Pray that you will be willing to follow Jesus wherever he leads you and whatever he wants you to do for him, both in the big decisions of your life and also in the events of the coming days.

Weekend

To see and contrast how another gospel writer has portrayed Jesus' last days, read Luke 22 – 24.

Memory verse: 'Then Jesus told him, "Because you have seen me, you have believed; blessed are those who have not seen and yet have believed"' (John 20: 29).

The uniqueness and ministry of Jesus

Everyone seems to be into symbols and logos these days. Coca Cola is recognizable almost anywhere in the world. You can tell it by the label. If Christians are identified by anything it is probably a rather gruesome form of torture and death. Not the guillotine or an electric chair, but a Roman form of execution, the cross. Why is this so important? Why should Christian faith centre on someone's death when it is supposed to be about giving life? Could God not have done things differently? Did Jesus *have* to die? To answer these questions we need to look at the uniqueness, firstly of Christ himself and secondly, of what he came to do for us.

> *Meekness and majesty,*
> *Manhood and deity,*
> *In perfect harmony,*
> *The man who is God ...*
>
> Graham Kendrick

The Man who is God

The uniqueness of Christ lies in the fact that he was both man and God. He was fully human. He was a

95

baby; grew up in a family; felt tired, hungry, thirsty; he had friends and wept when one died; he had arms, legs, eyes, just like us. He was God come down as man, whom we could identify with and understand.

He was fully God

Christ was God himself. As you read through John's Gospel, notice the things that mark Jesus out as being, at very least, extraordinary. He accepted worship; he fulfilled the Scriptures; he healed and performed miracles; he was totally sinless; he died an awful death but rose again – not mere resuscitation; his body has never been found. He still lives. No mere man could ever have done these things.

Why did Christ come?

Without Christ there is no Christianity and no hope for us to get right with God who created us. We are naturally separated from him and our sin is a big barrier between us. God's holiness and our sin just do not mix and we are as different as light is from darkness. Sin has to be punished – it offends God and actually makes him righteously angry.

But because God is wonderfully merciful he has taken the problem into his own hands and provided a way of escape. Only someone with no sin of his own and undeserving of death could pay for another's sins. No-one else fits the bill but Jesus. He came and lived in order to die. He was punished by God himself, not for his own sins, but for ours. We are familiar in football with the substitute who comes on to play when another footballer is injured or for some other reason cannot see the game through to the end. So we are unable to see life through to the end without either ultimately paying for our sins ourselves (that's what the Bible calls hell), or allowing Christ to be our substitute (in which case we go off the pitch of life forgiven!).

But what Christ did on the cross does not mean that the whole world is now automatically forgiven. Faith is involved. It is necessary to *believe* that what Christ did was for you. There is no blanket salvation without a personal repentance and faith.

> *It may be shocking. It may be incomprehensible. But it gives us a message to preach. God does not love us with beautiful, holy vagueness, but with a love that staggered under a cross, that was hung between thieves, that met and destroyed death and paid, to the full, our debt of sin.*
>
> John White, *The Race* (IVP)

WEEK SIX
PRAYER

A topic study

1. Jesus' handy hints

Matthew 6: 5-15

Jesus takes it for granted that his followers will pray.
He doesn't say, 'You must pray', but rather, 'When
you pray ...' (verse 5). If you stop and think about it,
that makes good sense – you can't imagine having to
tell an engaged couple that they must spend time
together because it should be their greatest delight.
In the same way we should delight in spending time
with our heavenly Father. But as in all relationships,
communication may need working at, and in this
passage Jesus gives his disciples some practical
hints to help them along.

99

1. *Before you study the passage, make a note of some of your prayers over the last five weeks which God has answered.*

_____

_____

_____

_____

_____

Look first at the prayer Jesus taught his disciples (verses 9-13). It's probably intended more as an example than a formula to be repeated by rote.

2. *How much of it is about God and how much about our own needs?*

_____

_____

_____

_____

3. *How close is your own praying to this pattern? Are there any aspects of this prayer that don't often feature in your prayers?*

_____

_____

_____

_____

_____

4. *Now go through the whole passage and make a list of other practical things Jesus tells his disciples about prayer. Do any of them answer any of your difficulties with prayer?*

_____

_____

_____

_____

_____

5. *Are there any practical changes you ought to make in the way you pray as a result of reading this passage?*

_____

_____

_____

_____

If you want to look at some more of Jesus' teaching about prayer, read Luke 11: 1-13. These verses have plenty of encouragement to ask God for all we need, both for ourselves and for others.

You probably had some difficulties with prayer that weren't answered by this passage. Take time to pray about them now – and remember, God wants you to enjoy prayer even more than you do, so it's a prayer you can reasonably expect him to answer! It would be good to look back at the end of this week and see if any more difficulties have been answered.

Other people's experience of prayer can be a great help, so why not find another Christian and discover how he or she prays? Also there are plenty of books on the subject. For something brief, practical and encouraging, try chapter 2 of *The Fight* by John White (IVP).

2. 'Let us praise the Lord'

Psalm 95

'Hallowed be your name' – praise comes right at the beginning of the prayer Jesus taught his disciples, and this psalm is a call to praise and worship God. And it's a call not just to an individual, but to a group of God's people – a reminder that prayer and praise is something we do with others, as well as on our own.

1. *From verses 1-7, make a list of reasons the psalmist gives for praising the Lord.*

_____

_____

_____

_____

_____

These are always causes for us to praise the Lord, even when life seems tough and it's hard to think of any other reasons.

2. *Can you think of any personal reasons for praising the Lord? Perhaps specific examples of the way he's cared for you (verse 7)?*

_____

_____

_____

The rest of the psalm is a reminder of occasions
when God's people disobeyed him (see Exodus 17:
1-7; Numbers 20: 1-13) with dreadful consequences.
True worship is more than honouring God by what
we say or sing. It also involves honouring him by
doing what he tells us (see Romans 12: 1).

When you come to pray, praise God for all that he
is and all he's done for you. Look back at your
jottings for reasons for praising the Lord, and make
them into your own prayer. You may like to sing to
God on your own. You may find it helpful to kneel, or
raise your arms in joy, or express praise through
other sorts of 'body language'. Take time as well to
ask God about anything he wants you to do (or not to
do) during the coming day, and pray you'll be ready
to listen and to do what he tells you.

3. Confession

Psalm 51

'Forgive us our debts' – Jesus expected his followers
to confess their sins and ask God's forgiveness, but
it's not always that easy. Facing up to our sin can be
a painful business, because we all like to think we're
basically nice people. Well, even the great heroes of
the Bible had the same problem, as you can see from
this psalm. David's sin had been flagrant – he'd slept
with another man's wife, then arranged to have him
killed in battle, to prevent him finding out that she

was carrying someone else's child (if you have time, read the whole story in 2 Samuel 11: 1 – 12: 25).

1. *How does David describe his sin (verses 1-5)? Does he make any attempt to excuse himself?*

_____

_____

_____

_____

2. *Go through the psalm and make a list of what David asks God to do for him.*

_____

_____

_____

_____

_____

_____

3. *What results does David expect from his prayer?*

_____

_____

_____

_____

_____

Note: In verses 16-17 David is well aware that there is nothing he can do to make amends for his sin to

God. All he can do is acknowledge his sin, the punishment it deserves (both adultery and murder carried the death sentence) and throw himself on God's mercy. From the New Testament we know more about how God can forgive our sin, yet still treat sin with the seriousness it deserves (we know instinctively that it wouldn't do for God simply to say that sin doesn't matter), because we know that Jesus is the one who takes our sin on himself (see John 1: 29).

This psalm should encourage you to be honest with God about your own sin and your need for forgiveness and restoration. As you come to pray, read through the psalm again, slowly. Are there any verses you particularly want to pray for yourself?

4. Thanksgiving

1 Samuel 1: 1 – 2: 11

Parents spend a great deal of time and energy trying to teach their children to say 'thank you' – but it's something adults find it easy to forget to say as well, especially to God.
    Start by reading chapter 1, to find out the circumstances of Hannah's prayer.

1. *What specific request does Hannah make to the Lord?*

_____

_____

_____

_____

2. *What was her response when the prayer was answered?*

_____

_____

_____

Now look in more detail at Hannah's prayer of thanksgiving, chapter 2: 1-11.

3. *Make a list of what Hannah says about the Lord in her prayer.*

_____

_____

_____

_____

_____

4. *Can you think of any prayers the Lord has answered for you in the last few days? What did you learn about God from them?*

_____

_____

_____

_____

5. *Look up Philippians 4: 6-7. Write out these verses below and try to learn them. Paul must have known they were true to write them, and they sum up Hannah's experience.*

_____

_____

_____

_____

_____

6. *Do you have any personal needs or anxieties at the moment? Ask God about them now. Make a note of any specific requests you make of him and make sure you remember to say thank you when you realize God has answered your prayers.*

_____

_____

_____

_____

Note: 1: 11 Uncut hair and beard was a sign that someone was dedicated to the Lord.

5. Praying for others

Philippians 1: 1-11

This letter was written from prison, where Paul was facing possible execution for his faith (Philippians 1: 13, 20). The church at Philippi had been started by Paul (you can read the story in Acts 16: 11-40), so he presumably knew it quite well. There are certainly hints in this letter that he knew of its current problems: disagreements among some of the members (*e.g.* Philippians 4: 2).

Think of a group of Christians you feel you should be praying for. It may be your own church, some other Christian group you belong to, or a church somewhere else with which you have prayer links. Think about this passage in the light of your prayers for them.

First concentrate on verses 3-8:

1. *What reasons does Paul give for praying with joy and thankfulness for the church at Philippi?*

_____

_____

_____

_____

2. *What is there to give thanks for in the situation of the Christians you pray for? Do any of Paul's reasons apply to them?*

_____

_____

_____

_____

Now go on to look at Paul's prayer in verses 9-11:

3. *What does Paul ask for this church? Try and write out the prayer in your own words, so that you explore the meaning of each phrase.*

_____

_____

_____

_____

_____

_____

Paul's prayer for love is obviously relevant to a
church trying to cope with disagreements among its
members, but he prays for more than a solution to
their immediate problems. He's also concerned for
their long-term spiritual growth.

4. *What particular problems or needs does the group
of Christians you're praying for face?*

_____

_____

_____

As you pray, don't forget these particular needs.
Jesus taught us to ask God for something as ordinary
as our daily bread, and Hannah's prayer yesterday
was concerned with an understandable human need.
But pray too for the spiritual growth of these
Christians. Try and write out a prayer that seems
appropriate, perhaps based on Paul's prayer, if that
fits the situation.

_____

_____

_____

_____

_____

Prayers in the Bible

The Bible is not like the 'holy books' of the world's religions, which ignore the historical setting and bypass the human writer. Instead, it is made up of different types of writing, such as history, story, practical teaching, wisdom literature and poetry. Many prayers are recounted in the Bible, including the 150 in the Book of Psalms. These are invaluable in showing us, as well as teaching us, about prayer.

For further reading: *People in Prayer* by John White (IVP) examines some of the prayers of the Bible in detail.

Weekend

Take a selection of psalms of your choice from the Book of Psalms, perhaps the first few. As you read them, recognize the different ways in which the psalmist prayed.

Spend time this weekend looking back over your notes from your studies of the last six weeks. What have you discovered about Jesus? What have you particularly learnt about being a Christian? Where do you go from here in growing as a Christian?

IVP has published several series of booklets similar to this one, such as the *Knowing God Bible Studies*. These aim to help you read the Bible with the purpose of enabling you to draw closer to God. Other series of booklets available from IVP are *Christian Basics*, *Fruit of the Spirit* and *The Beatitudes*. There are also many other materials to help you, some published by Scripture Union. A more experienced Christian friend or your local Christian bookshop will give you some ideas.

For details of daily Bible reading material, write to:

Scripture Union,
207 Queensway,
Bletchley,
Milton Keynes,
MK2 2EB.

What is Prayer?

Prayer. Try the word association game. What other words come to mind as you think about 'prayer'? Perhaps it's men in long robes chanting; God; hard on the knees; the Prayer Book; boring; what the minister does; asking for something; last resort. Prayer may have many different associations for you. It may be totally new and something you know that Christians do, but it all seems a mystery. How can God listen to my prayers if others are praying at the same time? Does he always answer? How do I learn to pray?

Is anybody there?

George Bernard Shaw once said, 'I know I'm God because when I pray to him I find I'm talking to myself.' So how will you know that you are not simply talking to yourself? Praying is not the power of positive thinking or a ritual routine. Neither is it constant repetition of words as if God is deaf! In fact it is not the performance of prayer which is the goal at all, but communication with God through prayer. A Christian wants to talk with God and prayer is the means. You can pray to God the Father through the Son and with the help of the Holy Spirit. In fact, the apostle Paul tells us in Romans 8: 26 that the Holy

113

Spirit will help you to pray, and Jesus himself prays for you. What prayer partners!

In another of the apostle John's writings, his first letter, he gives this promise about prayer:

> *This is the confidence we have in approaching God: that if we ask anything according to his will, he hears us. And if we know that he hears us – whatever we ask – we know that we have what we asked of him.*

1 John 5: 14-15

God promises that he will hear your prayers and you can have confidence that you are not talking to yourself. He will answer. Does that mean that you now have the key to everything you always wanted simply if you pray about it? Not quite! Remember that phrase, '*according to his will*'? Prayer must be a matter of finding out what God's mind is on something and praying with his best interests and glory at heart. It is not saying, '*my* will be done in heaven as *I* do it on earth', but, '*Thy* will be done on earth as it is in heaven.' You can find out what his will is primarily through Scripture. Thus, to take an absurd example, it is pointless to contemplate praying for God's help in murdering someone when God's own word clearly says, 'You shall not kill'!

But things are not always as clear-cut as that. The Bible will tell you all the main principles you need to live by, but it will not tell you where to go tomorrow, the name of the person you should marry, or whether you should be a doctor or a dentist. Prayer is asking what God's specific will is for you on such issues and entering into a dialogue with him whereby he can order your circumstances, guide you through other Christians and change your mind so that you start to think (and so to act) in a way that pleases him.

Does God always answer prayer?

Yes, God always answers prayer. But how? Does he always give us what we ask for?

Amy Carmichael, a missionary in India, used to pray as a young girl for blonde hair and blue eyes. She would wake up in the morning, dive expectantly for the mirror, and disappointedly find her normal dark hair and dark eyes. It was only in India that she realized and thanked God that her dark features blended with the Indians, where a blonde would have been out of place. Had God heard her prayer? Yes, but he knew far better what her real need was. You can be sure that God always hears and answers prayer. But the answer is not always 'yes'. Sometimes it is 'no' or 'wait'. Learn to trust him. It doesn't matter whether the issue is small or large. God is minutely attentive and delights in you talking things through with him.

There's more to prayer than asking

Prayer is not merely asking for things. It is the means of conversation with our heavenly Father. Any human father would be more than disappointed if his child used him merely as a dispensing machine to ask for things. Prayer is much broader. It involves *praising* God and adoring him for who he is; *confessing* whatever you have done wrong that has caused a barrier between you, and asking God's forgiveness; *thanking* God for what he has done in your salvation and in providing for you from day to day; *asking* – not only for yourself, but wider afield as well. A great privilege of prayer is being able to bring other people and situations to God and have the delight of seeing God answer.

Praying with others

Prayer is essentially the most intimate form of communicating with God. It may seem to be a purely private thing at first, especially as you learn to be real and honest with God.

But prayer is also a corporate act. In Acts 12: 12-17 many Christians had gathered together to pray for the apostle Peter's release from prison. They were praying so hard that they didn't believe it when Peter was miraculously let out of prison and stood knocking at their door! Christians have always met together to pray. Take opportunities to pray with other Christians. It may seem strange at first, but persevere. Your prayer need not be in a set form or any special language. It need not be long – one sentence will do if it is really from the heart.

PEOPLE AND PLACES IN JOHN'S GOSPEL

This is only a brief summary to give you an idea of the value of using a concordance or Bible Dictionary to add to your knowledge and understanding of what you are reading. All the material included can be found in the *Illustrated Bible Dictionary* (IVP), or in a concordance.

People

Andrew
One of the twelve apostles who came from Bethsaida in Galilee. He was a fisherman in partnership with his brother, Simon Peter (John 1: 35-44; 8: 9; 12: 21-22).

Annas
Appointed High Priest AD 6 and deposed AD 15, yet referred to as High Priest after that date (John 18).

Barabbas

Arrested for homicidal political terrorism, released as a substitute for Jesus (John 18: 40).

Caiaphas

Was High Priest AD 18-36, working in close co-operation with his father-in-law, Annas (John 11: 49; 18).

John, the Apostle

The son of Zebedee, brother of James, both of whom were in their father's fishing business in Galilee when Jesus called them. He is not mentioned by name in John's Gospel except as the son of Zebedee in John 21: 2, but he is most likely called the disciple whom Jesus loved (13: 23; 19: 26-27; 20: 2, 8). He is probably the author of this Gospel (John 21: 2).

John the Baptist

A cousin of Jesus who was called to be a prophet around AD 27. He quickly gained widespread fame as a preacher, calling for repentance and preparing the ground for Jesus. He died at the hands of Herod (John 1: 19-34; 3: 23-27; 5: 33-36).

Joseph of Arimathea

A secret disciple of Jesus who provided the tomb for him (John 19: 38).

Judas Iscariot

The disciple who betrayed Jesus, came probably from Kerioth, hence Iscariot. He was responsible for the finances of the apostolic band (John 6: 71; 12: 3-5; 13; 18).

Lazarus

Of Bethany, the brother of Martha and Mary (John 11; 12).

Martha

The sister of Lazarus and Mary of Bethany (John 11; 12).

Mary, the mother of Jesus

Not mentioned by name. John gives no details of Jesus' birth, but Mary is referred to in John 2: 1-11; 19: 25-26. ·

Mary

The sister of Lazarus and Martha, who is described as the one who anointed Jesus' feet with ointment (John 11; 12).

Mary Magdalene

Probably from Magdala in Galilee, from whom were cast out seven demons (Luke 8: 2). She was present at the cross and was the first to discover the empty tomb (John 19: 25; 20).

Nathanael

Seems to have been one of the Twelve, possibly being the same as Bartholomew. He was from Galilee (John 1: 45-51; 21: 2).

Nicodemus

A Pharisee and ruler of the Jews (John 3; 7: 50-52; 19: 39-40) (see Week 2: 1).

Pharisees

Religious leaders who genuinely tried to make the law bearable for the common man. They stressed individual fulfilment of all sides of the law.

Peter

From Bethsaida in Galilee, the son of Jonah. He was a fisherman with his brother Andrew. He was one of the first disciples to be called and was one of the three who formed the inner circle around Jesus (John 1: 41; 6: 68; 13; 18 – 21) (see Week 4: 5).

Philip, the Apostle

His home was in Bethsaida in Galilee (John 1: 43-46; 6: 5; 12: 21-22; 14: 8).

Pilate

Appointed as Roman prefect of Judaea in AD 26, he was in full control of the province. His powers included the reversal of capital sentences passed by the Jewish authorities. His relations with the Jews were poor (John 18; 19).

Thomas

One of the Twelve, he was a twin. Only in John's Gospel are there any personal references to him (John 11: 16; 14: 5; 20; 21: 2).

Places

Bethany

1. A village about 3 km (2 miles) from Jerusalem, the home of Lazarus.
2. A place beyond the river Jordan, unidentified, where John baptised (John 1: 28).

Cana in Galilee

A village in the uplands, west of the lake, mentioned only in John's Gospel.

Capernaum

The nearest village to the river Jordan on the north-west shores of the Sea of Galilee.

Sea of Galilee

A lake in the region of Galilee (also referred to as the Sea of Tiberias in John 21: 1). It is 21 km (15 miles) long, up to 11 km (7 miles) broad and lies at 211 m (692 ft) below sea level. The river Jordan flows through it from the north, so its waters are sweet, hence good for fishing. Surrounded by hills, it is liable to atmospheric down-draughts and sudden storms, *e.g.* John 6.

Jerusalem

A city at least 4,000 years old, established by King David as the capital of Israel, where his son, Solomon, constructed the temple. Both the temple and the city underwent periods of destruction and reconstruction. In 37 BC Herod the Great took control. He rebuilt the temple, this being the one in which Jesus taught. In AD 70 Jerusalem was virtually destroyed by Rome.

Judaea

The term used to describe all of Palestine, including Galilee and Samaria, or the area of Palestine which excluded these two regions.

Samaria

The capital of the Northern Kingdom of Israel before the Exile. The inhabitants of the area (Samaritans) had much in common racially and in religion with the Jews, but there was animosity between the two at the time of Jesus.